STEM Projects in MINECRAFT®

The Unofficial Guide to MINECRAFT® Agriculture

JILL KEPPELER

PowerKiDS press.

Published in 2025 by The Rosen Publishing Group, Inc.
2544 Clinton Street, Buffalo, NY 14224

First Edition

Editor: Greg Roza
Book Design: Rachel Rising
Illustrator: Matias Lapegüe

Photo Credits: Cover, p.1, 3–24 Soloma/Shutterstock.com; pp. 4, 6, 8, 10, 12, 14, 16, 18, 20 Levent Konuk/Shutterstock.com; p. 5 PhotoJuli86/Shutterstock.com; p. 17 Nattapon Ponbumrungwong/Shutterstock.com; p. 19 divedog/Shutterstock.com.

Library of Congress Cataloging-in-Publication Data

Names: Keppeler, Jill, author.
Title: The unofficial guide to Minecraft agriculture / Jill Keppeler.
Description: New York : PowerKids Press, [2025] | Series: STEM Projects in Minecraft | Includes index.
Identifiers: LCCN 2023052062 (print) | LCCN 2023052063 (ebook) | ISBN 9781499446906 (library binding) | ISBN 9781499446890 (paperback) | ISBN 9781499446913 (ebook)
Subjects: LCSH: Minecraft (Game)–Handbooks, manuals, etc.–Juvenile literature. | Agriculture–Juvenile literature. | Crops–Development–Computer simulation–Juvenile literature. | Wild plants, Edible–Identification–Juvenile literature. | Tree crops–Identification–Juvenile literature. | Fungi–Ecology–Juvenile literature. | Science projects–Juvenile literature.
Classification: LCC GV1469.35.M535 K4586 2025 (print) | LCC GV1469.35.M535 (ebook) | DDC 794.8/5–dc23/eng/20240105
LC record available at https://lccn.loc.gov/2023052062
LC ebook record available at https://lccn.loc.gov/2023052063

Manufactured in the United States of America

CPSIA Compliance Information: Batch #CSPK25 For further information contact Rosen Publishing at 1-800-237-9932.

Contents

Working the Land

The landscape of *Minecraft* is a huge one! As in the real world, there are many things in nature. There are crops you can plant to grow food and gain other resources, or useful things. There are wild plants that can help and sometimes hurt you. There are trees from which to gain building material. There are also other **dimensions** such as the Nether and the End.

Real-world STEM ideas having to do with **agriculture** also have an effect in *Minecraft*. Crops need irrigation, or water. Seeds need the right environment, or setting, to grow. It's important to know these things to succeed in the game.

MINECRAFT MANIA

There are different kinds of dirt in *Minecraft*. In addition to plain dirt blocks, there are grass blocks, farmland, dirt paths, rooted dirt, mud, mycelium (found only in mushroom fields), and podzol.

Most of the plants in *Minecraft* have real-world types too. This farmer is holding beetroots.

Minecraft Crops

Players can grow some in-game crops on farmland for food. You can create farmland by using a hoe on most kinds of dirt. Farmland that is soaked with water is called hydrated farmland. “Hydrated” means supplied with water. If there’s a water source within four blocks of the farmland block, it will be hydrated. Rain can also hydrate it.

Some crops only take up one block of farmland per planted seed or vegetable. These include beetroots and wheat (planted via seeds) and carrots and potatoes (planted via the vegetable itself). You can sometimes find planted crops and farmland in villages.

MINECRAFT MANIA

Players can get beetroot seeds by breaking beetroot plants in villages. They can get wheat seeds by breaking wheat plants in villages or breaking wild grass. Zombies may drop potatoes or carrots.

Since one block of water in *Minecraft* can hydrate four blocks to each side, one bucket of water poured in a one-block hole can hydrate 80 blocks of farmland.

Other crops include pumpkins and melons. Both come from seeds. These seeds grow a stem from the block where they're planted. The fruit, a full block itself, grows on one of the blocks next to the stem. Like other crops, both plants go through a few stages before they produce their crops. Melons drop melon slices. Pumpkins drop a full pumpkin block.

Crops take time to grow. However, you can make many plants grow faster by using bone meal on them. This is a **fertilizer** made from bones dropped by skeletons and other mobs.

MINECRAFT MANIA

You can find pumpkins growing in some village farms and in grassy **biomes**. Melons grow in the wild in jungle biomes. You might also find pumpkin or melon seeds in loot chests.

Minecraft villagers include farmers. These mobs will have composters you can use. Composters make bone meal from plant material (such as seeds) placed inside them.

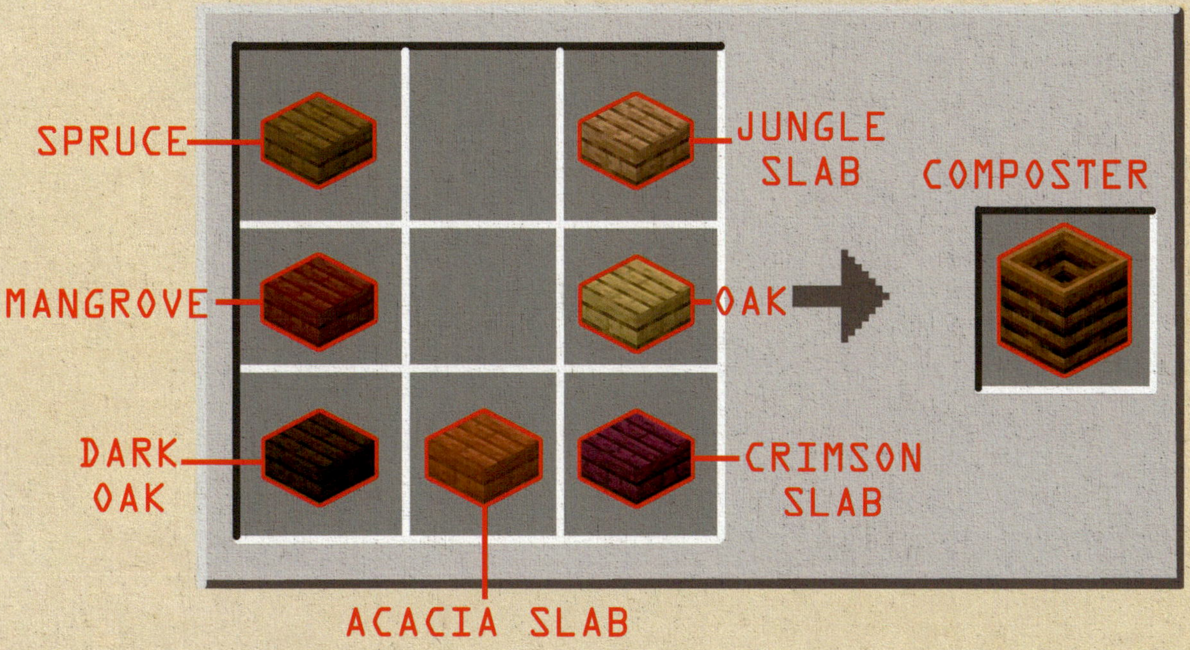

Wild Plants

Many plants grow wild in the *Minecraft* world. Grass grows nearly everywhere. Tall grass, ferns, large ferns, and vines grow in certain biomes. Sugar cane grows almost anywhere near water. Bamboo (jungles), cacti (deserts and badlands), lily pads (swamps), and sweet berry bushes (**taiga** biomes) have useful products or properties.

Lush caves are **unique** biomes in *Minecraft*. They're found underground, especially under more **humid** biomes like dark forests and jungles. Azalea trees often grow above them. Lush caves have unique plants and parts such as moss, azalea plants, cave vines, glow berries, glow **lichen**, spore blossoms, hanging roots, and dripleaf plants.

MINECRAFT MANIA

Azalea trees look a lot like oak trees in *Minecraft*. However, some of their leaves have pink-purple flowers. You can only grow azalea trees by using bone meal on an azalea plant.

Lush caves can include many resources found nowhere else. They also have unique mobs, such as axolotls.

A World of Color

Minecraft also has flowers. These come in many shapes and colors and grow on dirt and grass blocks. You can mostly use them for decoration but also to make dyes. Dyes are materials that you can use to change the color of other *Minecraft* items such as carpets, glass, and leather armor. There are 16 colors of dye available.

Different flowers grow in different biomes. They may be one block or two blocks high. One-block flowers include dandelions, poppies, blue orchids, alliums, tulips, and more. Two-block flowers include sunflowers (which always face east in the game), lilacs, rose bushes, and peonies.

MINECRAFT MANIA

Torchflowers, wither roses, and pitcher plants don't grow naturally. Torchflowers and pitcher plants can only be grown from seeds (or pitcher pods) found by the mob called a sniffer. Wither roses only drop when the wither mob kills another mob.

As in the real world, *Minecraft* bees **pollinate** plants. They will fly around flowers and collect pollen. Bees carrying pollen can drop it on crops, making the crops grow faster.

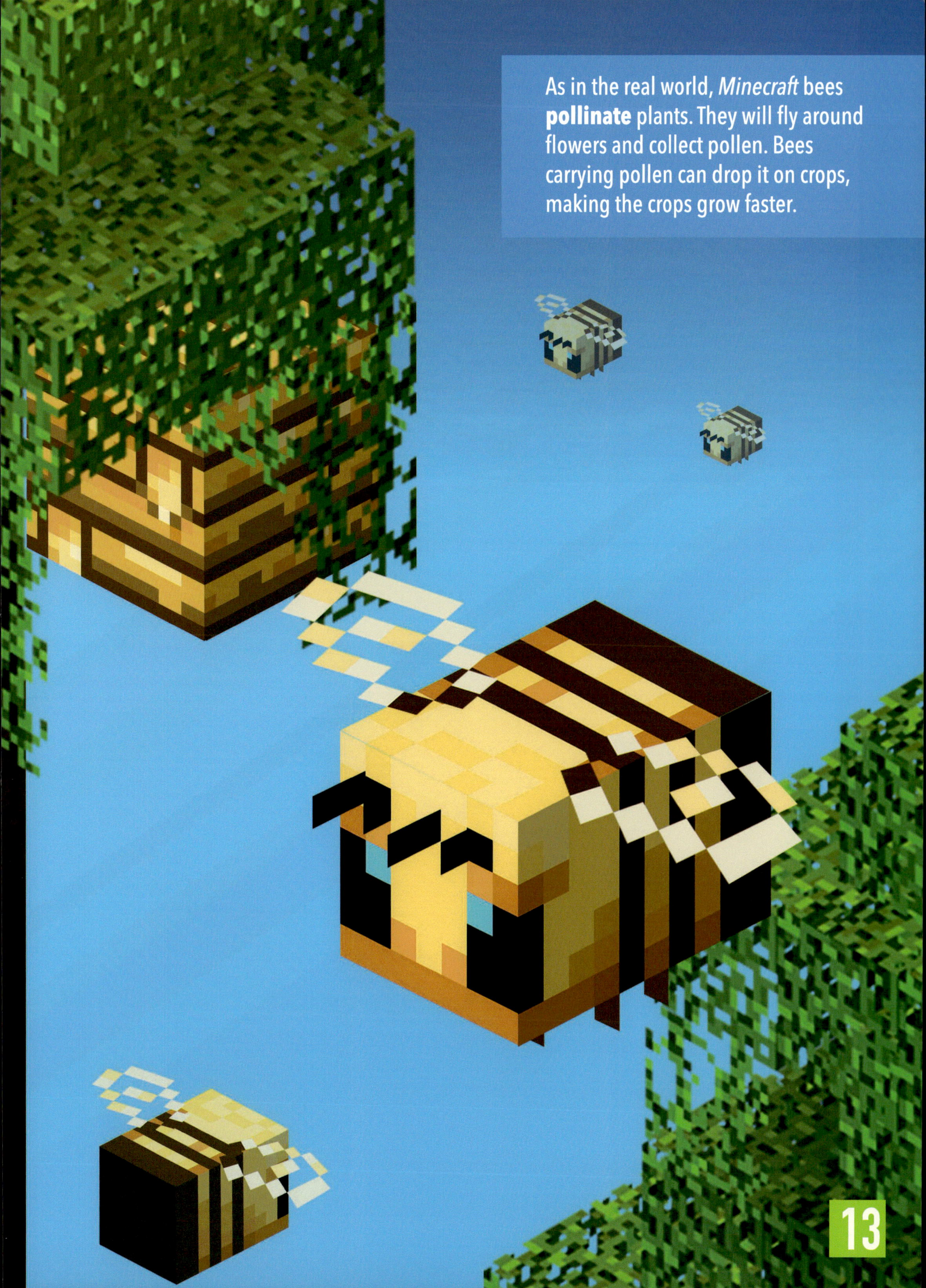

The Types of Trees

Minecraft trees are made up of log blocks and leaf blocks. A tree may be only a few blocks high or dozens of blocks high! Leaf blocks are arranged in different ways depending on what kind of tree it is.

Like other plants, different kinds of *Minecraft* trees grow in different biomes. Oak trees are the most common tree. Dark oak trees have darker wood and leaves and thicker trunks. Birch trees have white bark and paler wood. Spruce trees have several types and can be very tall, as can jungle trees. Acacia trees grow in savanna biomes.

MINECRAFT MANIA

Full-grown trees appear when a *Minecraft* world is created, but you can also plant them as saplings, or baby trees. They don't need water, but they do need light to grow.

Jungle trees can be very short or very tall. Some grow cocoa pods. Players can get cocoa beans from these.

Cherry blossom trees in *Minecraft* can only be found in cherry grove biomes. They have pink leaves. One unique thing about these trees and biomes is that cherry tree leaves drop pink particles, or very small bits of matter. Ground blocks in the biome may have pink petals on them.

Mangrove trees also have many unique aspects. They're only found in mangrove swamps. The trees have many leaf blocks and grow close together. Real-world mangrove trees often have prop roots and aerial roots, which are roots that grow above the ground. *Minecraft* mangrove trees have exposed aerial roots too.

MINECRAFT MANIA

In *Minecraft*, mangrove trees don't grow from saplings like other trees. They grow from propagules, which hang from mangrove leaves. Real-world mangroves also grow from propagules, which are like seedlings.

Real-world mangrove trees often grow in places with salty water.

Not Quite Plants

There are many living things that are much like plants—but not quite. The word "kelp" in the real world refers to many kinds of brown **algae** that grow in the oceans. Some kinds can be more than 200 feet (61 m) long! In the game, kelp grows in oceans too. It can grow to about 24 blocks tall.

There are many kinds of mushrooms in the real world. They're types of **fungi**. There are small red or brown mushrooms that grow in some *Minecraft* biomes. Unlike the real world, though, *Minecraft* also has huge mushrooms that can be as big as trees!

MINECRAFT MANIA

People may also think of corals as being like plants. They're really tiny ocean creatures that live in groups. Their hard skeletons form coral reefs. *Minecraft* also has coral reefs in warm ocean biomes.

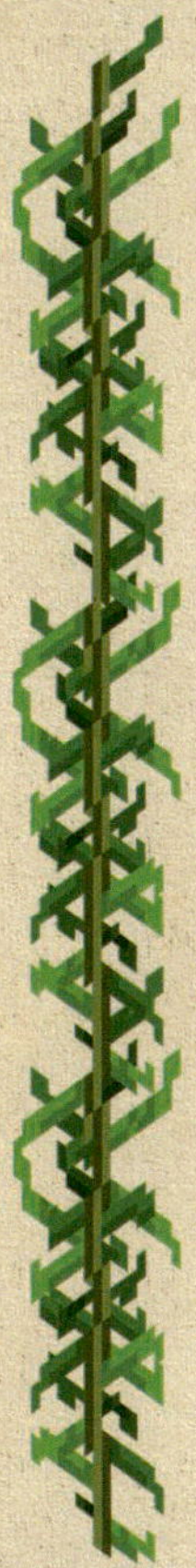

In *Minecraft*, you can collect pieces of kelp, dry them in a furnace, and eat them or make them into blocks and use them for fuel. Real-world people can also eat kelp or use it for fuel!

Nether and End

Minecraft also has dimensions called the Nether and the End. These areas have their own biomes and their own plants—or plantlike things. The Nether has a lot of fire and lava, or hot melted rock. It also has a few unique kinds of huge, treelike fungi and vines. Nether wart is another growth. It's important for making **potions**. You'll need to make a brewing stand to make potions.

The End has many floating islands in a dark void. On some of these islands, chorus plants grow. They look a bit like purple trees and grow chorus fruit and chorus flowers. If you plant one of the flowers on End stone, another tree will grow.

MINECRAFT MANIA

You can collect nether wart in the Nether and start crops of it in the *Minecraft* Overworld. But it will only grow on soul sand, which is also only found in the Nether.

You can find nether wart farms in nether fortresses, huge structures in the Nether.

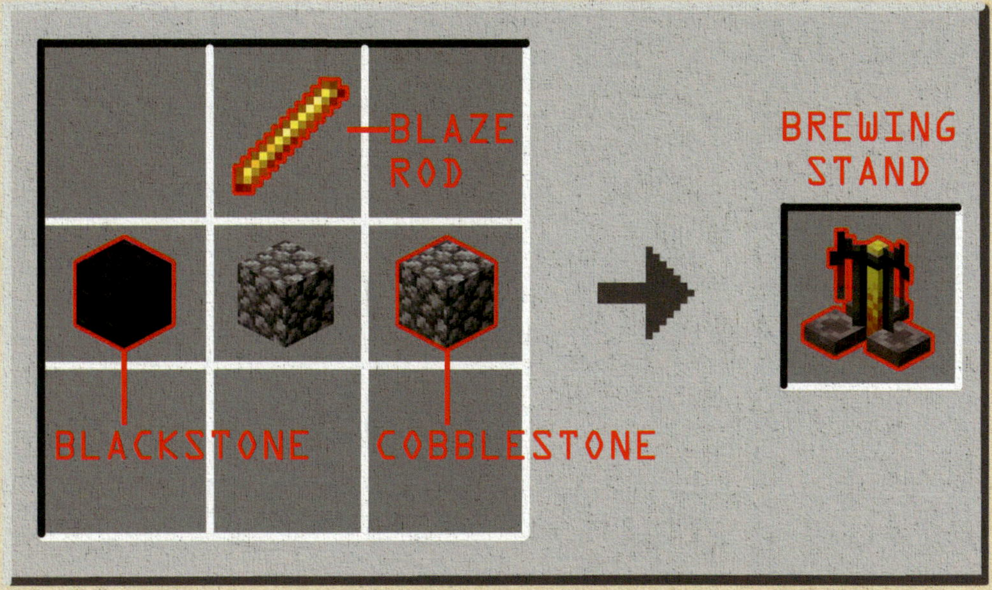

Glossary

agriculture: The science or job of farming.

alga: A member of a group of organisms called protists that mostly live in the water and use photosynthesis to make food like plants do. The plural is "algae."

biome: A natural community of plants and animals, such as a forest or desert.

dimension: A level of existence.

fertilizer: Something added to the soil to help plants grow.

fungus: A living thing that's like a plant but that doesn't have leaves, flowers, or green color or make its own food. The plural form is "fungi."

humid: Having a lot of humidity, or the amount of moisture in the air.

lichen: One of thousands of types of plantlike organisms that are part algae or cyanobacteria living among types of fungi.

pollinate: To take pollen from one flower, plant, or tree to another.

potion: A drink meant to have a magical effect on someone.

taiga: A biome that includes a humid, cold forest environment with many spruce or fir trees.

unique: Special or different from anything else.

For More Information

BOOKS

Biggs, Emma, and Steven Biggs. *Gardening with Emma: Grow and Have Fun*. North Adams, MA: Storey Publishing, 2019.

Mojang AB and the Official Minecraft Team. *Minecraft: Guide to Farming*. New York, NY: Del Rey, 2018.

Miller, Megan. *Minecraft Engineer: Must-Have Starter Farms*. New York, NY: Sky Pony Press, 2018.

WEBSITES

A Beginner's Guide to Farming in Minecraft
help.minecraft.net/hc/en-us/articles/360046311411-Minecraft-Farming-101
The *Minecraft* website helps with the basics.

Farming Guide
www.ign.com/wikis/minecraft/Farming_Guide
The IGN site provides more information on farming and agriculture in Minecraft.

How Do Plants Make Fruits and Vegetables?
wonderopolis.org/wonder/how-do-plants-make-fruits-and-vegetables
Wonderopolis answers this question and many more.

Publisher's note to educators and parents: Our editors have carefully reviewed these websites to ensure that they are suitable for students. Many websites change frequently, however, and we cannot guarantee that a site's future contents will continue to meet our high standards of quality and educational value. Be advised that students should be closely supervised whenever they access the internet.

Index